# Nods of approval for 'The Master Motivator'

***A compliment from 'The Father of Positive Thinking'***

If I wasn't feeling positive before, I am now! Dale is a great motivational speaker and has the ability to reach people and get them to make the most out of their lives.

*Norman Vincent Peale,*
Author of *The Power of Positive Thinking*
(One of Dale Brown's mentors)

***A well-received speech at the U.S. Naval Academy***

Coach Brown spoke at the Naval Academy while I was the Superintendent (President) there. The entire student body was in attendance.

His speech about "The Four Hurdles of Life" resonated strongly with our students, and was one of the best-received speeches during my time at the Academy. And that's saying something, given that his competition included President Clinton, Vice President Cheney, and Sheryl Sandberg.

The feedback I received was very positive, with many Midshipmen commenting on the Coach's ability to connect with the younger generation. It was a privilege having him on campus, and sharing his thoughts on Leadership, Perseverance and Integrity.

*Retired Vice Admiral Michael Miller,*
United States Naval Academy

### *Dale Brown was more than a basketball coach*

Coach Dale Brown was more than just a basketball coach – he was a mentor, a leader, and a man who understood that true success extended far beyond the court.

Like my mother, he instilled in me the belief that education was the foundation for a meaningful and impactful life. He always emphasized that the mind was just as powerful as the body, and that discipline, knowledge, and perseverance would open doors far beyond basketball.

Coach Brown is leaving a legacy that will always be cherished in the world of college basketball. A true mentor, motivator, and master of the game, he remains one of the most respected figures in college sports history.

What set him apart was his deep care for his players as people, not just athletes. He fought for us, defended us, and instilled in us the values of hard work, perseverance, and integrity. His influence went beyond the game, shaping young men into successful individuals both on and off the court.

His unwavering commitment to education and personal growth paved the way for me to become a successful neurosurgeon. The lessons he taught – about resilience, critical thinking, and striving for excellence – are the same principles that have guided me in the operating room, just as they once did on the court. Coach Brown didn't just develop great athletes; he shaped great men, teaching us that our potential was limitless if we were willing to put in the work. His legacy will always be one of inspiration, wisdom, and a deep belief in the power of education to change lives.

*Dr. Jason Cormier*
Lafayette, La.
(Former LSU basketball player)

(Editor's Note: Jason Cormier, M.D., who played basketball under Coach Dale Brown in the late 1980s, is recognized as one of the top neurosurgeons in the United States. An internationally renowned expert in traumatic brain injury and concussion, he's worked with organizations that include the NFL, NASCAR and NCAA football. He is a race car driver, book author, music producer and founder and CEO of the Motorsports Safety Group.)

### A 'riveting, electrifying' motivational talk

"Electrifying" is the way I would describe Dale Brown's magnificent speech I attended. He had the sizeable crowd on the edge of their seats. Having been employed by four of the top Fortune 500 companies in my 50 years in business, I've heard many motivational speakers, but none as riveting as his style and delivery.

*John L. Pavlish,*
Former master salesman

***Heads of state could learn from him***

Dale Brown is one of the most inspirational speakers and motivators I have ever heard or been around.

If heads of state throughout this troubled world had real concern and consideration for others as Dale Brown does, I doubt if our racial, religious and political problems would be a major issue. To him, all people are equal regardless of age, sex, position, race, or any other difference.

*Coach John Wooden (1910 - 2010),*
Former UCLA basketball coach
(One of Dale Brown's mentors)

# THE LITTLE BOOK OF MOTIVATION

Coach Dale Brown

Acadian House
PUBLISHING
Lafayette, Louisiana

The Acadian House Publishing Speakers Bureau can bring authors to your live event. For more information or to book an author, contact Acadian House Publishing at (337) 235-8851, Ext. 104, or info@acadianhouse.com.

ISBN 13: 979-8-9896580-8-4

---

**Library of Congress Cataloging-in-Publication Data**

Names: Brown, Dale, 1935- author
Title: The little book of motivation / Coach Dale Brown.
Description: Lafayette, Louisiana : Acadian House Publishing, [2025] | Includes bibliographical references and index. | Audience: Ages 13+ Summary: "A compact 112 page hardcover book packed with inspiring messages from one of America's top motivational speakers, former LSU basketball coach Dale Brown. The book is, essentially, a written version of some of Brown's most memorable speeches. Themes include courage, integrity, leadership, tolerance and teamwork. The author describes proven ways of achieving happiness, success and peace of mind"-- Provided by publisher.
Identifiers: LCCN 2025021521 | ISBN 9798989658084 cloth
Subjects: LCSH: Motivation (Psychology) Success--Juvenile literature | Leadership
Classification: LCC BF504.3 .B76 2025 | DDC 153.1/534--dc23/eng/20250610
LC record available at https://lccn.loc.gov/2025021521

---

- Published by Acadian House Publishing, Lafayette, Louisiana (Edited by Trent Angers; editorial assistance and research by Brooke Robin)
- Design and pre-press production by Jasmine Richard
- Printed by Sheridan Books, Chelsea, Michigan

*This book is dedicated to three women who have helped me to become exactly who I am:*

*My dear mother, Agnes, who was the most honest human being I have ever known and who provided for me under very difficult circumstances*

*My loyal wife, Vonnie, a great teacher, an independent spirit, always a steady source of common sense*

*My daughter, Robyn, so special and caring, an absolute blessing, who has brought so much joy into my life.*

## Foreword

# *Preacherman in tennis shoes*

My first encounter with LSU men's basketball coach Dale Brown came in 1979, when I met with him to discuss the creation of a brochure that would be used to recruit players for his team. I was in the advertising business at the time and went to see Dale at the suggestion of LSU's Athletics Director Carl Maddox.

Dale was a promoter by nature, and it's a good thing that he was. He had to do a lot of promoting to increase the size of LSU basketball's fan base. LSU has always been known as "a football school," and Dale was determined to build men's basketball from a mediocre team to a true national power. And he did, in the course of his 25-year tenure as head coach, beginning in the early 1970s.

As I was leaving that first meeting with Dale, he asked me a question that I couldn't have anticipated:

"Do you think you could help me get my TV show on the air?"

"I produce TV commercials. I've never produced a TV show before," I replied. "But, yes, I'll give it a try."

With that brief exchange, my life changed forever. I began a lifelong association with one of the most dynamic, positive-minded, highly motivated human beings God ever put on this earth – and I'm not exaggerating.

We started producing 30-minute television programs called "Inside LSU Basketball." The show was quite successful. We combined music with slow-motion basketball action and plenty of player smiles and laughter. We played the music of big name entertainers like Kenny Rogers, Wayne Newton and Barbara Mandrell. We never ran out of ways to surprise the fans. And Dale turned out to be a natural TV talent.

As time went by, Dale and I got to know one another well and became close friends. We developed a kind of "mind meld;" I could practically read his mind.

Then one day he called me with a most unusual invitation.

"I've got to go to Baghdad, Iraq, to help coach their national team to prepare them for the Arab World Games. Do you want to go?" he asked.

"Are you kidding me?" I replied as I processed this rare opportunity that seemed to come out of the blue.

He wasn't kidding. I accepted, and off we flew to Baghdad. It turned out that Iraqi players were noticeably different than U.S. players. For one thing, a couple of them came to the gym with big knives in their belts. That seemed more than a little odd, a local custom, I presumed. Also, when they got tired during practice they would just sit down on the floor and take a rest. Dale didn't try to correct them. I'm not sure how well they did in their big tournament as we headed home before the games began.

The trip to Baghdad was the first of many international escapades in which I accompanied Dale as he put on basketball clinics and gave motivational speeches. We did a lot of globetrotting, to France, Belgium, Germany, Singapore, Bangkok, you name it.

A recurring theme I heard in his motivational speeches was, "If you can believe it, you can do it." I also heard, "If you fix it in your mind, and you really want it badly enough, you can do it!"

A thousand times, when he was autographing a picture, or a basketball program, or just a piece of paper, he would add, "Never give up!" He was forever encouraging others to pursue their dreams, to keep fighting for what they believed in.

Dale Brown motivated his audiences at a deep level, pounding home the messages not only about tenacity but also about courage, self-determination, and the inherent worth and dignity of every human being. Those in attendance liked what they were hearing; what he was saying seemed to feed their souls. He had the undivided attention of practically everyone in the audience, including me.

Being there for his speeches motivated me and truly changed my outlook on life and the way I did business. I started believing that there was nothing I couldn't do if I set my mind to it. He awakened an entrepreneurial spirit that lay dormant somewhere in the back of my mind. So, halfway through my advertising career, I opened one of the nation's first cellular phone companies, then a potato chip company called Tiger Chips, then a courier business delivering documents. Then I got into the real estate business, first as a Realtor, then as a subdivision developer and homebuilder and finally as a real estate investor.

Dale is the one who convinced me that there was virtually no limit to what I could do in business:

"You can if you think you can."

He was right.

*—Jim Talbot*

(Editor's Note: Jim Talbot, who is longtime best friends with Coach Dale Brown, was Brown's driver and security guard for two decades or more, starting in 2000. They traveled together on dozens and dozens of trips throughout the U.S., Europe and the Middle East for Brown's speeches and basketball clinics. Talbot describes Brown as "the brother I never had."

Talbot heard so many of Brown's speeches over the years that he says he could give the speeches himself. Once, in New Orleans after Brown gave a rather long speech in the Superdome, Talbot asked him, "Do you know what part of your speech I liked best?" Expecting a compliment, Brown waited for Talbot to continue. Then Talbot said jokingly, "When you say, 'Now, in conclusion.'" They both got a good laugh out of that.

Talbot, a successful entrepreneur, homebuilder and real estate developer, serves as a City Councilman at Large for the newly incorporated city of St. George, which is adjacent to Baton Rouge.)

# Introduction

## *Words of 'The Master Motivator' on the printed page*

When Coach Dale Brown speaks, people listen.

It's not unusual for some in his audiences to take notes while others tape-record his speeches. Most seem to listen closely, not wanting to miss anything the man is saying.

On this particular day, in the summer of 2019 in New Orleans, Coach Brown will be addressing the Louisiana School Boards Association's annual convention. His keynote address is to be delivered in a large room that seats about 500 people. The room is filled to overflowing; it's buzzing with conversation.

Coach Brown ascends the steps to the stage. The master of ceremonies greets him, then proceeds to the podium to introduce him. The chatter of the audience subsides. Coach Brown begins to speak, and now the crowd is completely quiet. Not a word from them; you can hear a pin drop. There is obviously a high degree of respect for this man, bordering on reverence.

* * * * *

Dale Brown has long been recognized as one of the top motivational speakers in the nation. During the peak of his public speaking career, approximately 1982 through 2022, speaking invitations rolled in by the dozens in most years. They came from across town (Baton Rouge), across the state (Louisiana), across the nation and even from other countries, such as England, France, Argentina and Australia. The yearning for his encouraging words was widespread.

Many in his audiences, no doubt, wished they could have remembered much of what he said. And that's one of the purposes of this book: to create a written record of several of his most meaningful presentations.

For example, the ever-present need to stand up for what's right and just ("Evil prevails when good men do nothing."); the importance of teamwork over individual stardom, in business and in team sports ("The best version of 'me' is 'we.' "); and the need for integrity in one's pursuit of success and happiness ("To thine own self be true.").

These chapters offer a glimpse into the heart and mind of Dale Brown at his best and most inspiring: extolling the virtue of self-knowledge as a prerequisite to true success and peace of mind; and carefully articulating a message on the need for tolerance, suggesting how human beings should treat one another.

This book, like Brown's speeches, is a call to action. Noting that one person can make a difference – as history has shown – he points out that great social movements and subsequent reforms were started by the determined actions of small numbers of brave souls. He cites, for example, the abolition of slavery, the American civil rights movement, and the end to colonial rule over our country and others.

* * * * *

When Brown started coaching men's basketball at LSU in 1972, one of his stated goals was to build the weak LSU team into a true national power – and he succeeded. He brought his teams to the Final Four in 1981 and 1986; he captured the SEC Championship four times, and four times was runner-up; he won 448 games in his 25 years as head coach. He retired from coaching in 1997 as the winningest men's basketball coach in LSU history. In 2014, he was inducted into the National Collegiate Basketball Hall of Fame.

One of his greatest talents, besides his knowledge of basketball and coaching, was his extraordinary ability to motivate his players. He won many a game by convincing his team that victory was within their reach – even though the talent level of his players, in some cases, may not have been as high as that of their opponents. He practically *willed* them to victory in a number of games.

Observing this phenomenon, this nearly magic touch, courtside announcers and sportswriters started referring to Brown as "The Master Motivator."

And while the term originated in the sports world, it caught on and began to be used in the public speaking arena as well. It was used routinely when he was being introduced before his speeches

– to trade associations, the military, and all manner of civic and religious groups.

Indeed, Brown's reputation preceded him. Those who came to hear him generally understood he was a highly effective motivational speaker, someone whose speech would lift their spirits, someone whose message would nourish their minds and souls and build their self-confidence. This is what many expected, and this is what Brown delivered consistently.

* * * * *

Little wonder that Brown's talks were inspiring, considering the three men who served as his mentors starting when he was in his thirties. One was Dr. Norman Vincent Peale, "The Father of Positive Thinking" and author of the international bestselling motivational book titled *The Power of Positive Thinking*. Another was legendary UCLA men's basketball coach John Wooden – a man filled with wisdom, compassion, humility and an unshakable religious faith – whose character is described in some detail in a chapter in this book.

The third was Pastor Bob Richards, a California theology professor and Olympic Gold Medalist in pole vaulting. He was one of the absolute best, most inspiring speakers the world had ever heard. He taught Coach Brown some of the secrets of effective public speaking: talk to the audience in a way that is helpful to them; make it about them and their needs; build them up; lift their spirits; speak with energy, with conviction.

Clearly, Dale Brown owes these three men a debt of gratitude – a fact that he happily acknowledges. No doubt, they contributed significantly to the making of one of America's top motivational speakers.

–*Trent Angers*
(Dale Brown's biographer)

## Prologue

# *Lessons my mother taught me*

Two days before I was born, my father left my mother and me and my two sisters, ages 11 and 12, and he never returned. His departure put my mother in a difficult position.

She had an eighth-grade education, came off the farm in North Dakota, and couldn't get a job during the Great Depression in 1935. She had to do several things that were unpleasant for her: she became a babysitter and cleaned people's houses, and she had to put our family on welfare.

We lived in a one-room apartment above a bar and hardware store, and I remember my mother getting a monthly check of $42.50 from Ward County Welfare. She would sit down and meticulously decide what food she could buy for the coming week.

More than once during these difficult times she taught me lessons that have stayed with me my entire life. From her, I learned honesty, courtesy, and consideration of others. She was a model of courage and tenacity.

I saw her put on her winter coat, walk down a flight of stairs, and take back to the Red Owl and the Piggly Wiggly grocery stores 25 cents and 40 cents because the clerks had given her too much change for the groceries she bought.

My mother was graceful and modest. She followed the advice of St. Francis of Assisi, who said, "Preach the gospel every day, and if necessary use words." That's how she taught us many of life's lessons: by her actions, by her example.

Not once did I hear her talk negatively about the man who walked out on us and never returned, never sent any money, never wrote. She didn't drink, smoke, swear, speak badly about anyone, or ever date anyone. She never seemed to be bitter or angry, and I never heard her complain about her situation in life.

My mother's Catholic faith seemed to be unshakable. She brought me to Mass and Communion daily – not just on Sundays, but daily. For me, the daily trip to church was a ritual. To my numerous fake illnesses and attempts to get out of going, my mom's response was always the same: "Get up, son. We're going to church."

Being a small place, our apartment was uncomfortable and cramped. It never provided any place for me to get away on my own. So, at night I often went outside to sit on the fire escape above the alley. One night I'll never forget, when I came back in from sitting out there, my mom asked me to sit in her little rocker. She pulled up the footstool and we talked.

"I am embarrassed to tell you this," she said, "but it is something you should know. When people come to pick me up to go babysit, I am so embarrassed about our situation that I look up big words in the dictionary, and then all the way to their house I inject these big words into our conversation to try to impress them. That's called making an image.

"If you spend too much time polishing your image, you'll eventually tarnish your character and be an unhappy man."

That night, my mom taught me that being my true self was far more important than trying to impress people or pretend to be someone I was not. The lesson here is that your character is who you really are, and your image is what you are perceived to be.

I believe that if William Shakespeare were around today he would agree wholeheartedly, considering the famous line he wrote in the play, *Hamlet*:

"To thine own self be true. And it must follow, as the night the day, thou canst not then be false to any man."

This is one of the guiding principles I've tried to live by my entire adult life. I highly recommend it as a prerequisite to true happiness and peace of mind.

*– Dale Brown*

# Contents

# THE LITTLE
# BOOK OF
# MOTIVATION

*You must have eagerness to sacrifice personal interests or glory for the welfare of the team.*

– John Wooden (1910 - 2010)
Renowned UCLA basketball coach

# 1

# 'No man is an island'

## (We're all in this together)

Even when I was a young man playing high school sports in Minot, North Dakota, I heard it said often that one player can make a big difference, but a team working in unison can make a miracle.

That was true then, and it's true today. It applies not only to building a sports team but also to building a community or a business.

None of us got to where we are today without the help of others. The late, great Chicago Bears running back Walter Payton (1953 - 1999) knew this to be true. He said:

"My father told me it is your responsibility, once you've had some success, to reach back and bring someone with you. He said if I was fortunate enough to experience success, then I made it because others helped me along the way. Someone gave to you. That's why it is your job to give back. Too many of us only take. We don't give."

Anything is possible when we come together and cooperate and put aside petty differences; the results can be astounding. For instance, the United Nations estimates that poverty has been reduced more in the past 20 to 30 years than in the previous 500 years. This goes to show that when we work together we can solve any problem.

We are all component parts of a great whole, dependent on each other for our very existence.

Seventeenth century British poet John Donne nailed it when he wrote:

> No man is an island, entire of itself; every man is a piece of the continent, a part of the main. If a clod be washed away by the sea, Europe is the less. ... Any man's death diminishes me, because I am involved in mankind. And therefore never send to know for whom the bell tolls; it tolls for thee.

Pastor and civil rights leader Martin Luther King made the same point when he wrote:

> All people in this world are tied into a single garment of destiny. Whatever affects one directly affects all indirectly. ... We are made to live together and help each other.

Noted British writer Rudyard Kipling (1865-1936) addressed the power of unity when he wrote:

> Now this is the Law of the Jungle – as old and as true as the sky; and the Wolf that shall keep it may prosper, but the Wolf that shall break it must die. ... For the strength of the Pack is the Wolf, and the strength of the Wolf is the Pack.

Unity involves a devotion and dedication to a cause which brings everyone closer together. When an individual loses himself in a cause that's greater than himself, he and the whole team emerge as winners.

I'm totally convinced that we are capable of solving any problem, whether it be poverty, racism, crime, pollution, terrorism, or whatever else plagues humankind. What's required is our commitment, determination, and perseverance – propelled by the boldness of faith.

Now is the time to make a commitment to make the world a better place to live.

*I know of no more encouraging fact than the unquestionable ability of man to elevate his life by conscious endeavor.*

— Henry David Thoreau

*Everything can be taken from a man but one thing: the last of human freedoms – to choose one's attitude in any given set of circumstances, to choose one's own way.*

— Viktor Frankl (1905 - 1997)
Austrian psychologist, philosopher and Holocaust survivor
Quoted from his book, *Man's Search for Meaning*, based on his experiences in Nazi concentration camps

# 2

# The power to choose

## (The greatest of powers)

The only constant in life is change. Nothing is permanent, yet we are programmed to wish it were. We all want life to feel safe and secure, and permanence gives us the illusion that it is.

The more we push for permanence in life, the more we set ourselves up for disappointment when we find it is not achievable to the extent we think it should be. But when we accept the fact that change is inevitable, and adjust for it, we are on the road to happiness and success.

In the midst of turbulence, it is natural to dwell on the negative – which is not in our best interests and can be crippling. When your life is in turmoil it's easier to eat badly, not exercise, sleep poorly, drink too much, feel lethargic, and allow your mind to be filled with negative thoughts.

Such thoughts often give way to fear – real, gut-wrenching fear that can paralyze a person and distort his or her outlook on life. This is why Henry David Thoreau, the noted nineteenth century writer and philosopher, wrote, "There is nothing to fear but fear itself." (Thoreau's quote, which appeared in his 1851 journal, became widely known when it was repeated by President Franklin Roosevelt in 1931 during his first inaugural address, and in 1961 by President John Kennedy.)

Fear is a crippling, negative emotional state characterized by a heightened sense of agitation, tension, doubt and anxiety. When we let fear take over our minds we are affected in a variety of ways:

• We avoid difficult or uncomfortable situations. (If we don't confront these challenges we can never move past them.)

• We inhibit ourselves – which results in things getting worse.

• We fixate on the past – which often brings on feelings of guilt.

• We develop a fear of failure, embarrassment, and losing control.

Fear can create the illusion that things are worse than they actually are. Indeed, FEAR is the acronym for "False Evidence Appearing Real."

All of us will face critical moments in our lives when decisive action and courage are needed. Courage sustains us in the face of difficulty and gives us the strength to persevere boldly to face uncertainty and fear. Without courage we can't practice any virtue consistently.

Anyone can look good after a big financial gain, a promotion or an award, but how will we react to being demoted, fired, bankrupt, divorced, addicted, or being diagnosed with a serious illness? Your Failure Quotient – the ability to bounce back after life's disappointments and setbacks – is far more important than your Intelligence Quotient. Your FQ will sustain you during the roughest of times.

The greatest power in the world is our power to choose how we react to the problems of life. We don't want to be someone who lives a life of excuses and negative thinking. The person who really wants to improve his or her life finds a way to do so and not an excuse.

If Henry David Thoreau were alive today he'd agree wholeheartedly. He wrote:

"I know of no more encouraging fact than the unquestionable ability of man to elevate his life by conscious endeavor."

* * * * *

Some people look for obstacles in every opportunity while others look for opportunities in obstacles. Life has no remote control; you have to get up and change things yourself. Now, to propel your dream forward you must have intuition, imagination, determination, courage, and the boldness of faith. And, remember, it is never too late to become what you might have been if you are ready to adapt to change and accept the challenges that confront you. Don't be someone who lives a life of excuses instead of action.

Excuses are like belly buttons: everyone has one. To move from victim to victory a person must change his or her attitude. A bad or defeatist attitude is like a flat tire, until *you* change it you are not going anywhere.

My mother taught me that if you are looking for a helping hand, look at the end of your own arm. Each of us is responsible for the person we become.

It is easy for us to allow circumstances to control our lives, or we can learn to control our circumstances and make things happen for the better.

You, and you alone, are responsible for your future. You are really free the moment that you do not look outside yourself for someone to solve your problems. You will know that you are on the right path when you no longer blame anyone or anything but realize you control your own destiny.

In our journey of life each of us roams the earth with our own special uniqueness. We are all different, but there are two things we all have in common. First, we will constantly be facing adversity. There will always be struggles to overcome. Second, we each have the ability to respond in any way we choose. There are always solutions, and it takes brave souls to search for them. Each and every day we are faced with some form of challenge. However, our ability to overcome those challenges, no matter their size, lies directly with our ability to choose how we will respond.

*The only thing necessary for the triumph of evil is for good men to do nothing.*

– John Stewart Mill (1806 - 1873)
English philosopher

*You're betraying your whole life if you don't say what you think – and you don't say it honestly and bluntly.*

– Charles Krauthammer, M.D. (1950 - 2018)
American syndicated political columnist
Harvard-educated psychiatrist

# 3

# Standing up to evil requires courage

Moral courage made this the greatest country in the world. It enables us to stand up for what we know is right – even if it means standing alone and risking rejection or other negative consequences.

Whenever there is a lapse in moral courage, evil always perpetuates itself. When good and evil compromise, evil always wins.

Martin Luther King once asked a question that should stop us dead in our tracks:

"Why is it that the children of evil and darkness are always much more aggressive and vociferous than the children of light and goodness?"

The world can be a dangerous place to live, not only because of the people who do evil things, but because of all the people who don't do anything to counter that evil.

Courage sustains itself in the face of difficulty and finds the strength to persevere boldly to face danger, threats, uncertainty, fear and intimidation. Maya Angelou defined courage perfectly when she said:

"Courage is the most important of all the virtues, because without courage you can't practice any other virtue consistently. You can practice any virtue erratically, but nothing consistently without courage."

It is easy to come up with a litany of excuses for not being courageous, but until we are fully committed there will always be hesitancy to act.

We are really free the moment that we stop looking outside ourselves for someone else to solve problems. We must be the change we wish to see. The idea of saviors has been built into our culture. We have learned to look to others, thus surrendering our own strength, demeaning our own ability, and causing us not to act.

Great social transformations such as the end of

slavery, the women's and civil rights' movements, and the end of colonial rule all began with public awareness and engagement. A small number of courageous and committed people led the way to freedoms we all enjoy today.

English philosopher John Stuart Mill (1806 - 1873) warned us about apathy and inaction:

"The only thing necessary for the triumph of evil is for good men to do nothing."

Any system that is totally dysfunctional and evil can be cleansed only by courage and commitment to see goodness prevail.

"I learned that courage was not the absence of fear, but triumph over it," Nelson Mandela wrote.

So the question in our journey of life is not whether God can bring peace into the world and move us forward. The question is: *Can we?*

The answer is *yes*, if we are fully committed, disciplined, courageous, and possess a powerful faith. The boldness of faith is so powerful that nothing can stop it. It is the spinal cord to everything in our life, but we must have the courage to use it.

In each of us there are heroes. Speak to them and they will come forth and stand for justice and freedom.

*He has achieved success who has lived well, laughed often and loved much; who has gained the respect of intelligent men and the love of little children; ... who has accomplished his task and has left the world better than he found it.*

– Bessie Anderson Stanley (1879 - 1952)
American writer and poet

# 4

# The search for success and happiness

How do we find success and happiness?

It can be difficult because we have distorted the true meaning of success. In 1806, the dictionary described it as "fortunate, happy, kind and prosperous." Now, the dictionary describes success as "attainment of wealth, fame, rank and power."

This modern-day message bombards us every day from every direction, and we tend to believe we can't be successful or happy unless we attain these things.

Surely we must guard our minds against the illusion of success. To build lives that are meaning-ful and fulfilling, we must understand that so much of our lives can be consumed with things that are not critical for our happiness. The more we are connected to the illusion of success, the further we will be from ever finding true happiness.

So, what can we do to find success and happiness? First, we must get over the four major hurdles of life – the common things that trip up so many people. We can get past these obstacles if we have the commitment and discipline to really want to do it; a feeble effort to improve will fail.

## Hurdle #1 – 'I can't / You can't'

Most of us don't scratch the surface of our potential. If we did all the things we are capable of doing, we would literally astonish ourselves.

Hold on to the image of the life that you want and that image will become a reality. Always remember, whatever your mind can conceive and believe it can achieve. Don't procrastinate. Take immediate and massive action.

It's easy to come up with a litany of excuses. Don't ever sell yourself short by underestimating your ability.

A good example of a young man who didn't

accept his high school coach's evaluation of him is Shaquille O'Neal, who later became a basketball superstar at LSU and in the NBA. He was cut from his high school team and told he was too slow, too clumsy and had too big of feet and should try out to be a soccer goalie.

The lesson here is clear: Don't let anyone control your destiny – except you. Remember and take to heart the words of the poem, *Invictus*:

"I am the master of my fate, I am the captain of my soul."

## Hurdle #2 – Past failures or fear of failure

Historically, success often follows a series of failures. Success can be built on multiple failures. Take, for instance, Thomas Edison. It took him more than 1,000 attempts to get the light bulb to function. He said:

"The most certain way to succeed is always to try just one more time."

Don't lose faith in yourself. Faith can calm the stormy seas of our lives; the boldness of faith is so powerful that nothing can stop it.

Resist being a pessimist. Replace negative

thoughts with positive ones. Open your mind to your limitless potential, and you will be surprised by the results.

History provides us with numerous examples of highly successful people who lived through many failures, but they still made their dreams come true. Our response to failure determines our future.

J.K. Rowling, the famous author of the *Harry Potter* series, said:

"I failed on an epic scale. An exceptionally short-lived marriage had imploded, and I was jobless, a lone parent and as poor as it is possible to be ... without being homeless. I was the biggest failure I knew. ... You will never truly know yourself, or the strength of your relationships, until both have been tested by adversity."

Being a success has little to do with the judgment of so-called experts. So, the next time an expert criticizes or scoffs at your dream, you can take comfort in realizing that people who achieved some of the greatest accomplishments in the world were told that their goals were impossible. (A word to the wise: Keep away from those who belittle your dreams.)

When we do experience failure in our jobs or

in our personal lives we must not shackle ourselves with guilt – because guilt can lead to the suffocation of the spirit. We can become ineffective because of unresolved guilt. We have to let it be over and done with or it can destroy our self-esteem.

The lack of self-forgiveness can fester like a poison within us and can cause anxiety, depression and illness. If you are going to live a truly productive life, you have to forgive yourself and quit beating yourself up with the thoughts of "I should not have done that or I could have done better." As Oscar Wilde wrote:

"Every saint has a past, and every sinner has a future."

Every day in some way our courage will be tested, but remember that adversity only visits the strong but stays forever with the weak. It is your choice whether to be bitter or better.

## Hurdle #3 – Handicaps

Most of us have handicaps of one kind or another. And we must realize that to overcome them it's not our background but our backbone that counts.

Handicaps aren't only of the physical nature but also psychological, emotional, financial, and circumstantial. Oprah Winfrey is a perfect example. She was born to an unmarried teenage mother, lived in extreme poverty and abuse, and was pregnant at age 14.

She had every reason to give up and yet she overcame these handicaps through determination and "by the grace of God." Her triumph over nearly impossible odds should give us all hope that the impossible is what nobody can do until somebody does it.

### Hurdle #4 – Lack of self-knowledge

The beginning of wisdom is being honest with oneself. The most noble and perfect victory is the triumph over oneself. Only the truth about yourself can set you free and relieve you of self-doubt.

Self-knowledge requires putting in the time to ponder the big questions of life. And this means spending time away from the busyness of the workaday world – possibly while making a retreat, possibly on a long drive alone, or a leisurely walk on a country road.

Down through the ages, great thinkers have

carved out time for contemplation, including Harvard Business School professor Clayton Christensen. When he was a college student, he spent time daily thinking about his destiny and expanding his self-knowledge. He wrote in the *Harvard Business Review*:

> I decided to spend an hour every night reading, thinking and praying about why God put me on this Earth. ... I stuck with it and ultimately figured out the purpose of my life. ... My purpose grew out of my religious faith, but faith isn't the only thing that gives people direction.

Knowing who we are in relation to our Creator is, of course, an indispensable component of self-knowledge. Why are we here? What is my main purpose for being here, in this town, in this country, in this family? Is it true that there is life after death? Among those who pondered questions such as these for much of his adult life was Henry David Thoreau, the American philosopher and poet. He wrote:

> I know that I am. I know that another is who knows more than I, who takes an interest in me, whose creature, and yet whose kindred in one sense, am I.

Another great thinker who addressed the subject of self-knowledge in the spiritual realm was the Native American Indian called Yellow Hawk. In his *Prayer to the Great Spirit*, he wrote:

> Oh, Great Spirit, whose voice I hear in the winds, and whose breath gives life to all the world, hear me.
>
> I come before you, one of your children. I am small and weak. I need your strength and wisdom.
>
> ... Make my hands respect the things you have made and my ears sharp to hear your voice. Make me wise, so that I may know the things you have taught my people and the lessons you have hidden in every leaf and rock.
>
> I seek strength, not to be superior to my brothers, but to be able to fight my greatest enemy, myself. Make me ever ready to come to you with clean hands and straight eyes, so when life fades as a fading sunset my spirit may come to you without shame.

As we go about our lives here on earth, the truth is that no amount of wealth, accomplishments or credentials can substitute for peace of mind and knowing oneself.

There is a choice we have to make in everything we do. So keep in mind that in the end, the choices we make, make us.

We have unlimited potential, and if we keep our feet planted in common sense and never give up, then, with God's help, we will find true peace, success and happiness.

*Someday, after mastering the winds, the waves, the tides and gravity, we shall harness for God the energies of love, and then, for a second time in the history of the world, man will have discovered fire.*

– Pierre Teilhard de Chardin, S.J.
Jesuit priest and philosopher

# 5

# The virtue of tolerance

Prejudice keeps us from moving forward because it enables us to form opinions of other people without bothering to learn anything about them. It's a lame rush to judgment, a mentally lazy way of relating to others.

A perfect example of this occured in 1857 when the U.S. Supreme Court issued the infamous Dred Scott decision in which it declared that Black people in the United States, whether slave or free, could not be American citizens.

American writer and philosopher Napoleon Hill many years later wrote a superb piece on prejudice and intolerance.

> When the dawn of intelligence shall have spread its wings over the eastern horizon of progress, and ignorance and superstition shall have left their last footprints on the sands of time, it will be recorded in the book of man's crimes and mistakes that his most grievous sin was that of intolerance.
>
> The bitterest intolerance grows out of racial and religious differences of opinion as the result of early childhood training. How long, dear God, until we poor mortals will understand the folly of trying to destroy one another because of dogmas and creeds … .
>
> … I am hoping that I will find no Jews, Gentiles, Catholics, Protestants, Germans, Englishmen, Frenchmen or Russians, Blacks or Whites, Reds or Yellows when I shall have crossed the bar to the other side.
>
> I am hoping that I will find there only human souls, Brothers and Sisters all, unmarked by race, creed or color, for I shall want to be done with intolerance so I may lie down and rest, … undisturbed by strife, ignorance, superstition and petty misunderstandings … .

To live by relying on one another implies a risk, but without some trust in humanity life would be unlivable.

One of our greatest national leaders, Abraham Lincoln, said:

"If you trust, you will be disappointed occasionally, but if you mistrust, you will be miserable all the time."

Lincoln's point is well illustrated in part by this poem by James Patrick Kinney:

**The Cold Within**

Six humans trapped by happenstance
In bleak and bitter cold
Each one possessed a stick of wood,
Or so the story's told.

Their dying fire in need of logs,
The first man held his back
For of the faces around the fire
He noticed one was black.

The next man looking 'cross the way
Saw one not of his church,
And couldn't bring himself to give
The fire his stick of birch.

The third one sat in tattered clothes,
He gave his coat a hitch.
Why should his log be put to use
To warm the idle rich?

The rich man just sat back and thought
Of the wealth he had in store.

And how to keep what he had earned
From the lazy, shiftless poor.

The black man's face bespoke revenge
As the fire passed from his sight,
For all he saw in his stick of wood
Was a chance to spite the white.

The last man of the forlorn group
Did nought except for gain.
Giving only to those who gave
Was how he played the game.

Their logs held tight in death's still hands
Was proof of human sin.
They didn't die from the cold without,
They died from the cold within.

* * * * *

One Christmas a Jewish friend of mine sent me a Christmas card and it was titled "Was Jesus Crazy?"

> He came into the world with the nutty idea that human beings could love one another ... . Peace on earth indeed... . We cannot love one another. The best that we can do is keep the levels of hatred low enough, so we don't exterminate one another.
>
> It was a great idea, of course; too bad that it didn't work.
>
> Still ...What if he wasn't crazy? What if he

> was right? What if it was possible to love one another? What if the lion can lie down with the lamb? What if Arab and Jew, Protestant and Catholic, black and white, young and old, male and female can love one another without fear, without hatred, without death and destruction? What if life does triumph over death, light over darkness, good over evil, love over hate... ?

Of course, love will triumph over hate, and tolerance can overcome intolerance. But we've got to work at it.

The world-changing power of love was addressed eloquently by the French Jesuit priest and philosopher Pierre Teilhard de Chardin (1881 - 1955). His words are unforgettable:

> Someday, after mastering the wind, the waves, the tides and gravity, we shall harness for God the energies of love, and then, for the second time in the history of the world, man will have discovered fire.

Impossible? Not at all. I'll say it again: The impossible is what nobody can do until somebody does it!

*I expect to pass through life but once. If therefore, there be any kindness I can show, or any good thing I can do to any fellow being, let me do it now, and not defer or neglect it, as I shall not pass this way again.*

– William Penn (1644 - 1718)
English writer and founder of Pennsylvania

# 6

# We must all learn to live together

The Boston Celtics pro basketball team is a paramount example of what can happen when people work together. This is one of the greatest dynasties in the history of sports. They have won 18 NBA Championships.

Now, some years ago another Boston pro team, the Boston Red Sox, held a fellowship breakfast at Fenway Park. Rabbis, priests, ministers and civic leaders gathered in ecumenical fashion to extol the virtues of brotherhood. At one such conclave the Red Sox general manager addressed the group. He said:

"You are sitting in a sports building talking about brotherhood. May I suggest that the best example is right down the street from here? There's a team over there in the Boston Garden, made up of whites, blacks, Catholics, and Protestants, coached by a Jew, and they've been World Champions for a long time now. Everyone's running around looking for theories and searching into history for explanations. If you want a perfect example of what we have been talking about, just look at the Celtics."

The harmony and mutual respect alluded to are part of the beauty and mystery of the Celtics empire. But unfortunately we are letting virtues such as these slip away from us these days. It's clear to me that we need an open and honest conversation on race relations in our country.

It's also clear that education, open-mindedness and tolerance are needed in order to make this world a better place for all of us. There is no limit to what we can achieve as a society when we cooperate and work together for the common good.

The burdens of racial discrimination and oppression have been borne historically in this country not only by African Americans but by Native American Indians as well.

From the 1770s to the present time there were some 370 treaties that were ratified between the American Indians and the U.S. government, and shamefully the government has violated provisions in the majority of them. Yet, the two words the American Indians have waited patiently to hear – "We're sorry" – have never been spoken officially by the government.

Today on the reservations, alcohol, drugs, suicide, babies with no fathers, rape and inferior education are all part of the long trail of tears for these neglected, abused and forgotten Americans.

African Americans have suffered unfairly through 250 years of slavery, 90 years of Jim Crow laws, 60 years of separate-but-equal, and years of racist housing policy. Until we recognize and admit this, America will never be whole.

Now, to anyone who would claim not to be aware that racism is still raising its ugly head in our country, you would have to be in a coma! To solve the problem both parties must admit their flaws.

Black people all over our nation fear the violent, dysfunctional behavior that has made murder by other black males the number one cause of death for black males between the ages of 15 and 34.

Ninety percent of young black men who are killed are killed by other black men.

What helps to perpetuate the problems in the African American community is that 70 percent of all births are out-of-wedlock. And nearly 70 percent of these children are growing up in single-parent households.

Education is another major problem. Less than 50 percent of black males graduate from high school, and 75 percent of crimes are committed by high school dropouts.

The connection between crime and low educational achievement by some in the black community is especially tragic – and undeniable. There is a direct correlation between low reading scores in grammar grades and criminal behavior later in life. Those who plan and build prisons study the reading levels of fourth grade boys to calculate how many prison cells they will build in 10 to 20 years. This unhappy fact of life is stunning and depressing; it's as though some young people are predestined to spend at least part of their lives in prison.

* * * * *

Martin Luther King, a man with great strength and wisdom, made many profound statements in his day. In one, Dr. King said:

"We must never struggle with falsehood, hate and malice. We must never become bitter. There is a danger that those of us who have been forced so long to stand amid the tragic midnight of oppression – those of us who have been trampled over, those who have been kicked about – there is a danger that we will become bitter.

"But if we will become bitter and indulge in hate campaigns, the new order which is emerging will be nothing but a duplication of the old order. Riots cannot win and their participants know it. Hence, rioting is not revolutionary but reactionary and invites defeat and futility.

"Change can happen only through education, justice and unity. As long as the mind is enslaved, the body can never be free. No Emancipation Proclamation, no Civil Rights Bill can totally bring this kind of freedom. Man will be free only when he reaches down to the inner depths of his own being ... and signs his own emancipation proclamation."

Another black leader, Nelson Mandela, spent 27 years unfairly imprisoned in South Africa, and in 1994 he was elected President of that country. The day he became President, he said:

"I stand here before you not as a prophet, but as a humble servant of you, the people. I have paid the price for forsaking some of life's pleasures to give freedom to the black people of South Africa; however, we must now stress discipline, education, and respect to one another if we are ever to truly be free. ... Education is the most powerful weapon you can use to change the world."

No doubt, the keys to moving from victim to victory and injustice to justice are education, discipline, commitment, respecting each other, doing your very best, and being honest with yourself. Nothing is so beneficial as a true knowledge of oneself.

Man can fly faster and higher than any bird in the history of the world; he can dig deeper and longer into the earth than any burrowing creature.

The only thing man hasn't learned to do is walk on earth in peace and harmony with his fellow-man. When we do this, when we move forward with moral courage, we will make the world a much better place for everybody.

*There is so much frustration in the world because we have relied on gods rather than God. We have genuflected before the god of science only to find that it has given us the atomic bomb, producing fears and anxieties that science can never mitigate. We have worshiped the god of pleasure only to discover that thrills play out and sensations are short-lived. We have bowed before the god of money only to learn that there are such things as love and friendship that money cannot buy.*

– Dr. Martin Luther King Jr. (1929 - 1968)
Baptist minister and American civil rights leader

# 7

# The importance of spiritual formation in families

I don't profess to be an expert, but as a coach and teacher for 44 years and as a parent and grandparent, I asked myself what values or virtues were the most important to me in guiding young people.

And I came up with quite a list. But the two that stand out for me as the foundation of a healthy spiritual life are love and faith.

Without love there can be no compassion, patience, generosity, or loyalty.

Without faith there can be no courage, persistence, discipline or hope. Faith is what binds us together. It directly affects how we view ourselves and how we will understand what it takes to obtain true peace of mind. Some put their faith in financial security. Others seek peace in continual activity. Others look for it in human friendship or adulation. These things are not the source of true peace.

A daily life of straight thinking and unselfish following of God's will are the only sources of true peace. Dr. Martin Luther King had this to say on the subject:

"There is so much frustration in the world because we have relied on gods rather than God. We have genuflected before the god of science only to find that it has given us the atomic bomb, producing fears and anxieties that science can never mitigate. We have worshiped the god of pleasure only to discover that thrills play out and sensations are short-lived. We have bowed before the god of money only to learn that there are such things as love and friendship that money cannot buy."

* * * * *

## Sermons We See

By Edgar Guest

*I'd rather see a sermon*
*than to hear one any day.*
*I'd rather you should walk with me*
*than to merely tell the way.*
*The eye is a better pupil*
*and more willing than the ear.*
*Fine counsel is confusing,*
*but example's always clear.*
*The best of all the preachers*
*are the ones who live their creeds.*
*For to see good put in action*
*is what everybody needs.*
*I soon can learn to do it*
*if you'll let me see it done.*
*I can watch your hands in action,*
*but your tongue too fast may run.*
*And the lecture you deliver*
*may be very wise and true,*
*but I'd rather get my lessons*
*by observing what you do.*

Down through the ages parents have realized that their children tend to model their behavior after them. Parents are, by and large, their children's role models, for better or for worse. The American novelist and essayist James Baldwin (1924 - 1987) observed in one of his insightful essays in the 1960s:

"Children have never been very good at listening to their elders, but they have never failed to imitate them. They must, [because] they have no other models."

**Children Learn What They Live**

By Dorothy Law Nolte

*If children live with criticism,*
*they learn to condemn.*

*If children live with hostility,*
*they learn to fight.*

*If children live with ridicule,*
*they learn to be shy.*

*If children live with shame,*
*they learn to feel guilty.*

*If children live with tolerance,*
*they learn to be patient.*

*If children live with encouragement,*
*they learn confidence.*

*If children live with praise,*
*they learn to appreciate.*

*If children live with fairness,*
*they learn justice.*

*If children live with security,*
*they learn to have faith.*

*If children live with approval,*
*they learn to like themselves.*

*If children live with acceptance and friendship,*
*they learn to find love in the world.*

As with any journey, sometimes the sheer magnitude of parenting can overwhelm us. But remember, the journey is comprised of many small steps filled with bumps in the road along the way. However, if you remain grounded in common sense and surrender yourself to love and faith, then you can find true success and lasting peace in your family.

**How to train your child to be a delinquent**

By Charles R. Swindoll

*When your kid is still an infant, give*
*him everything he wants. This way, he'll*

*think the world owes him a living when he grows up. You cannot help others by doing for them what they can and should do for themselves.*

*When he picks up swearing and off-color jokes, laugh at him. It won't take long before his mouth gets him into trouble.*

*Never give him any spiritual training. Wait until he is 21 and let him decide for himself.*

*Avoid using the word "wrong." It will give your child a guilt complex. You can condition him to believe later.*

Faith and love are what ground us and set us free to live a truly authentic and peaceful life. A human being without faith, or reverence for anything, is a human being morally adrift. As parents, teachers, and mentors our most important mission in this life must be the spiritual formation of our children. It is our job to ground them with the necessary ethical and moral foundations – not only with our words, but more importantly by our actions.

In order to be good parents, we must first know and accept ourselves. As psychologist Carl Rogers puts it:

"To accept ourselves: Therein lies the source of genuine freedom. [But if] we do not accept ourselves, we cannot be really free, especially in our relationships."

In accepting ourselves, we are accepting God's unconditional love for us. When we surrender ourselves to God's love and will, we will discover true peace and happiness. This surrender, this connection, is essential to the spiritual formation of our families.

Among those who have addressed this all-important subject is Saint Teresa of Avila, a sixteenth century Carmelite nun and Spanish mystic. She put it this way:

> *God alone should be the epicenter of our lives, the heart of our existence, the soul of our actions, and we dare not accept any fraudulent substitute or we will be incomplete as a human being.*

That's good advice, sister – one of those eternal truths that has stood the test of time.

*The longer I live, the more I realize the impact of attitude on life. The remarkable thing is that we have a choice every day regarding the attitude that we will embrace for that day. ... I am convinced that life is 10 percent what happens to me and 90 percent how I react to it. ... We are in charge of our attitude.*

– Charles Swindoll
Christian pastor and radio preacher

# 8

# Caring for our bodies, minds and spirits

Aging is inevitable but the rate of aging is not, and living longer does not have to be about "taking longer to die."

Health experts say we have the ability to live considerably longer and healthier if we just take some basic and simple steps. These include:

• Restrict calories.

• Consume proper foods. Eat more fruits and vegetables and cut out the bad fats.

• Increase strength by exercise and weight lifting.

• Exercise your mind by reading, among other things.

- Get quality sleep.
- Control anger, stress, and worry.
- Eliminate smoking.
- Control alcohol consumption.
- Choose the right doctor and be honest with him or her. Don't be macho. (In 44 years as a coach I've dealt with many doctors, and I find most to be talented, caring, good listeners, and positive-minded.)

I personally feel we must also educate ourselves and take control of our own health. Your health is your responsibility, not your doctor's or anyone else's. Be knowledgeable about the use of vitamins, herbs and medicines being prescribed to you.

Maintaining a positive outlook is one of life's great challenges and one of life's great opportunities. Having a purpose – a higher meaning to one's life than mere existence – is a critical part of one's overall health.

A 35-year study at Harvard University showed that people with a pessimistic outlook on life suffered significantly more disease after age 45 than people with a positive outlook. As Winston Churchill once wrote:

"An optimist is one who sees an opportunity in every difficulty, and a pessimist is one who sees a difficulty in every opportunity."

Dr. Larry Dossey, in his book *Healing Words: The Power of Prayer and the Practice of Medicine*, describes one of the best-kept secrets in medical science: the benefit of prayer. He explains:

"Prayer is a powerful and legitimate method of healing, and scientific data supports the efficacy of spirituality in the healing process."

Pastor Rick Warren, author of *The Purpose-Driven Life*, wrote a profound article about life after his wife was diagnosed with cancer. He wrote:

"We aren't going to live forever, and this life is just a preparation for eternity. Life is a series of problems: You are in one now, you're just coming out of one, or you're getting ready to go into another one. So, you can focus on your purposes, or you can focus on your problems."

Pastor Warren also offers this wise counsel:

*During difficult times–Seek* God.
*During painful moments–Trust* God.
*During happy moments–Praise* God.
*During quiet moments–Worship* God.
*During every moment–Thank* God.

Norman Cousins served as Professor of Medical Humanities for the UCLA School of Medicine, where he did research on the biochemistry of human emotions. Believing that emotions can be the key to success in fighting illness, he wrote:

"A new branch of medicine – psycho-neuroimmunology, which deals with the interactions between the brain, the endocrine system and the immune system – is producing some shocking answers.

"Intense determination and hope, it has been discovered, can have a major physiological effect by stimulating an increase in red blood cells and a corresponding increase in the number of cancer-fighting cells which can destroy cancer cells ... . In combination with the powerful advances of modern science, those forces can make a significant difference in the patient's ability to overcome illness."

* * * * *

This generation of children is the first ever with a life expectancy lower than that of their parents. In the U.S. today, nearly 75 percent of adults are obese or overweight. There are 300,000 deaths a year in our nation from obesity-related causes.

It's clear that our attitudes toward life and health can improve our days on this earth and extend our life expectancy considerably.

Pastor Charles Swindoll wrote a superb piece on the importance of attitude, including a bit of wisdom we should all take to heart:

"The longer I live, the more I realize the impact of attitude on life. The remarkable thing is that we have a choice every day regarding the attitude that we will embrace for that day. We cannot change our past. The only thing we can do is play upon the one string that we have and that is our attitude. I am convinced that life is 10 percent what happens to me and 90 percent how I react to it. And so it is with you. We are in charge of our attitude."

In my opinion, many of our health problems are an outward manifestation of a much larger problem. That is, we live in a gluttonous, lazy, self-indulgent, television-addicted, pill-popping society.

We must act now to improve our lives and our children's lives. The late UCLA basketball coach John Wooden said it so well:

"Make a decision! Failure to act is often the biggest failure of all."

*In order to be a leader a man must have followers. And to have followers a man must have their confidence. Hence, the supreme quality for a leader is unquestionably integrity. Without it, no real success is possible, no matter whether it is on a section gang, a football field, in an army or in an office. ... His teachings and actions must square with each other. The first great need, therefore, is integrity and high purpose.*

– Dwight D. Eisenhower,
President of the United States, 1953 - 1961
U.S. Army General and Supreme Commander
of Allied Expeditionary Forces in Europe in
World War II

# 9

# How to be a top-flight leader

## 15 notable characteristics of great leadership

During my most active years as a college basketball coach and public speaker, I met and spoke with some truly remarkable leaders in the U.S. and abroad.

Since then, I've come to the conclusion that top-flight leaders come in all shapes and sizes, with personalities ranging from the quiet and scholarly to the loud and easily excitable. I noticed, too, that many of these leaders seemed to share several of the same characteristics: courage, integrity, self-confidence and vision, to name but a few.

### 1. Vision

Through the ages a common quality of great leaders is they have been masters of articulating an appropriate vision of the future. They see things that are not yet there and have the ability to relay this vision to others. Those who are able to see the invisible are now capable of doing what many may think of as impossible. But remember, the impossible is what nobody can do until somebody does it!

### 2. Teamwork

Nothing significant can ever be accomplished without team unity. The most important aspect of your job is getting your team to work together – and to fully understand that *the best potential of ME is WE.* Convince them that an individual can make a difference, but a team can make a miracle happen. Teamwork doesn't just happen; it takes a trusted leader to give the organization direction, purpose and ultimately success.

Effective leadership depends on your ability to connect with and motivate people – not based on your title, position or power, but on their trust and respect for you.

### 3. Recruiting

The ability to recruit the best talent possible is imperative for success in all businesses. You must recruit well to remain competitive.

To be successful, a leader must develop a core of loyal staff members who share his sense of mission.

Make sure you are on the same page from the beginning regarding values. These values must include what is right, fair, honest and legal.

You have to go through a lot of rocks to find one gem. Find people who already have a pattern of success, loyalty, discipline and ethics. Be cautious of recommendations.

Weak leaders surround themselves with weak people. The mark of a gifted leader is to pick people who are smarter than him in his weak areas.

### 4. Effective communication

A series of interviews with some of America's most successful business leaders found that almost all of them, when asked what they considered the primary reason for their success, said that their ability to communicate was their greatest asset.

The late UCLA basketball coach John Wooden said:

"There's a big difference between knowing what you are doing and knowing how to communicate what you know."

Make it crystal clear what is expected. Research shows that most people will remember only 50% of information received after 10 minutes and only 10% after 24 hours. So use simplicity with constant repetition, as Coach Wooden advised frequently.

**5. Accessibility**

If you set yourself off behind closed doors, chances are that your team members won't feel comfortable coming to you. However, if you involve yourself and provide accessibility, you will then have your finger on the pulse of the office or the team.

**6. Be a good listener**

Many leaders do not understand this concept very well, because they are doing most of the talking. Take a sincere interest in what others are saying.

Listen for ideas and feelings. Your being a good listener will help others to build their self-confidence and realize they are important and appreciated.

## 7. Keep them informed and check on progress.

Put checks in place to monitor progress toward goals and get feedback from your team. A real leader is interested in finding the best way to accomplish goals and not necessarily in having his own way.

## 8. Congratulate and encourage

Praise produces positive results. But remember, constant praise loses its effectiveness.

Know the difference between flattery and sincere appreciation. Flattery comes from the mouth while appreciation comes from the heart. One has selfish motives, while the other does not. One is cloaked in exaggeration, and the other is dressed in truth.

Contrary to what we have heard often, research indicates that higher salaries, long paid vacations and plush offices are not as important as a person feeling wanted, appreciated, respected, involved and being a part of a family.

William James, one of the greatest philosophers this country has ever produced, said:

"The deepest craving of human nature is the need to be appreciated."

It is important to reinforce your communication with praise for a job well done. Nothing is a bigger motivator than people feeling good about themselves. That isn't to say that you shouldn't critique or evaluate a poor performance.

However, you can't load up a person with negative comments and expect him to change his behavior. Encouragement is the seed of inspiration. By encouraging a person, it lets the person know that you have faith in his or her abilities.

**9. Set a good example and ask yourself some questions.**

*What are my work habits like?*

*Am I consistent?*

*Do I admit my mistakes?* Worthy leaders take full responsibility.

*Do others believe in me?* They depend on you to stand the test of pressure. No leader is exempt from criticism, and his humility will nowhere be seen more clearly than in the manner in which he accepts and reacts to criticism.

*Do I delegate properly?* Your most precious resource is time, and if it is squandered on tasks that can be carried out by others, your effectiveness will be reduced.

*Do I welcome spirited debate?* All major problems

should be brought to the leader's attention. However, insist that when this is done that at the same time recommendations are made for solving problems. A leader with followers who always agree with him reaps the counsel of mediocrity.

*Am I too soft?* At times you must fire people, either for incompetence, laziness, dishonesty, disloyalty or insubordination. It is never pleasant, but sometimes it is just the tonic an organization needs. Weak leadership and a refusal to confront problems rapidly lead to decay.

### 10. Deal with various egos

As a leader, you will have to deal with incredible egos and delicate egos. How you work with the various egos is a unique art.

### 11. Set a standard of accountability

Expect results. Low expectations result in low production. Don't only expect but inspect. Do not tolerate excuses or the transferring of blame.

### 12. The art of self-motivation

- Refuel your mental tank daily.
- Begin each day with reflection, prayer and exercise.

- Enthusiasm is contagious! Do you have a positive mental attitude?
- Be passionate. You have to love what you do.

**13. Be honest, humble and sincere**

Humility is such a vital ingredient in being a great leader, yet it is such an elusive virtue. Great leaders never take themselves too seriously.

Be sincerely interested in those with whom you work. Remember, people want to be understood and appreciated. If there is the slightest doubt about whether you care for their well-being, then your leadership efforts will be in vain. It's true: People don't care how much you know until they know how much you care.

Only by understanding and caring for people can you motivate them to achieve their potential.

**14. Mental toughness**

Stay focused.

Don't major in minor things.

Prioritize: Do things in order of their importance.

Be a problem solver. Turn your obstacles into possibilities or opportunities.

Be confident in your decision-making.

## 15. Know yourself

What is your purpose or mission in life? Is it selfish or selfless?

Be honest with yourself about your strengths and weaknesses.

If your personal life is at peace, then chances are your professional life will be, too.

Many leaders have lost their moral compass amidst the materialism and greed of our times. Imagine how differently businesses would function if the power of goodness and doing things fairly replaced the power of money and cheating people.

No doubt, the world desperately needs great leaders. Great leaders fill you with hope and shower you with a thousand reasons to embrace life.

You can make a real difference through your leadership and fierce determination.

*America will never be destroyed from the outside. If we falter and lose our freedom, it will be because of our own apathy.*

– President Abraham Lincoln, 1861 - 1865

# 10

# We need statesmen representing us, not politicians!

Never have I seen the American public so disgusted and fed up with our Congress. Partisan politics, negative campaigning, and one scandal after another is literally sickening our people.

It is clear to me that we must cleanse a system that is totally dysfunctional and out of control. There's no doubt that we have lost our moral compass.

Far too many politicians don't measure up to their self-righteous rhetoric. We need to hold them accountable by voting them out of office.

Correcting any problem begins by facing it head on and not hiding behind partisan politics or political correctness. We have a right to demand candidates who will lead – and at the same time listen to we the people who elect them. As Thomas Jefferson said:

"The federal government is our servant, not our master."

Samuel Adams, one of our Founding Fathers, wrote:

> If ever a time should come when vain and aspiring men shall possess the highest seats in government our country will stand in need of its experienced patriots to prevent its ruin.

Public awareness and action to demand change is the only method of preserving our freedoms. Now is that time because Congress has become a haven for far too many narcissistic politicians for whom self-promotion, self-preservation and greed have taken over.

**God bless America, but wake up America!**

You might be asking yourself: *What can little ole me do?* Just remember, nobody makes a greater mistake than he who would do nothing because he could do only a little. For far too long we have looked to others to solve the problems of our country, and that's not working.

Great social transformation – such as the end of slavery, the women's and civil rights movements and the end of colonial rule – all began with public awareness and engagement. These movements were started by the determined actions of small numbers of courageous and committed citizens.

Have you ever noticed that if any one of us lies to Congress, it's a crime? But if any one in Congress lies to us, it is just considered politics as usual. Frankly, I believe candidates from both parties have lied to the American people. It has become standard operating procedure for many politicians to say whatever is necessary in order to get elected. This must stop.

Ronald Reagan acknowledged the problem when he said:

"Politics is supposed to be the second-oldest profession. I have come to realize that it bears a very close resemblance to the first."

If we don't demand honesty and integrity from America's leadership now – and reward that integrity with our votes – our leaders will lack the fortitude to make the hard decisions that must be made to change course.

Our nation is in a state of crisis, and we need to

change before it is too late to choose the direction of that change.

We need the best possible people in office to make this happen. Many of them, of course, are already in office, but they need our help to surround them with men and women who will do what they know to be right and true.

* * * * *

We the people are responsible for the character of our Congress. If that body is ignorant, reckless, or corrupt, it is because we tolerate ignorance, recklessness, and corruption. If it is intelligent, brave, and pure, it is because we demand these high qualities in our representatives.

I have traveled in 90 countries throughout the world and fully realize there is no better place to live than the USA. I feel so blessed to be an American citizen. However, I have never seen the American public so angry and frustrated with our leaders. We are to blame for many of our current problems because we have not demanded enough from those that represent us.

So now the question is: *Can we change a system that desperately needs change?* The answer is emphatically *yes*, but only if we are vigilant, committed and courageous enough to demand good ethics and honorable leadership.

If we do not act now, what Abraham Lincoln said (in essence) can surely happen:

"America will never be destroyed from the outside. If we falter and lose our freedom, it will be because of our own apathy."

Let's take some action now to demand change. Let's stand together with renewed confidence and determination that we can make a difference. The easiest path is to think someone else will get it done, but that will not happen.

We must create the changes we wish to see.

*At the end of life, we will not be judged by how many diplomas we have received, how much money we have made, or how many great things we have done. We will be judged by "I was hungry, and you gave me something to eat. I was naked and you clothed me. I was homeless, and you took me in."*

– Mother Teresa of Calcutta

# 11

# A role model for the ages

My dear friend Coach John Wooden of UCLA basketball fame was my mentor for nearly 40 years. He was the wisest and most genuine human being I have ever known.

Not only that, but he was highly intelligent, kind and principled – in a word, a role model for this and every generation.

Why was the greatest basketball coach who ever lived like this and not egotistical, selfish, arrogant and greedy, like so many who reach the pinnacle of what the world often defines as success?

I believe it is because he marched to the beat of a different drum. He thought of success in a way that didn't include conventional goals such as wealth, fame and power.

"Success is peace of mind that is a direct result of self-satisfaction in knowing you made the effort to become the best you are capable of becoming," Coach Wooden said.

Numerous times I was with him, and someone would shower him with praise. His reply was always the same:

"Thank you, that is so kind of you, but I am still a work in progress. I imagine that I am neither as good as some people think nor as bad as some others consider me to be. Perhaps I am more like the one who said, 'I am not what I want to be, not what I am going to be, but I am thankful I am not what I used to be.'"

Coach Wooden was loaded with wisdom and was the humblest man I ever met. When he retired at UCLA in 1975, after 27 years and 10 National Championships, his salary was only $32,000 per year. He told me he never asked for a raise.

His coaching philosophy included a principle I'll never forget:

"Coaching out of fear is temporary; coaching out of love is permanent."

He was a very spiritual man. He stated profoundly:

"There is only one kind of life that truly wins, and that is the one that places faith in the hands of God. Until that is done, we are on an aimless course that runs in circles and goes nowhere."

I heard him mention on several occasions that he believed that the four things people crave the most are freedom, happiness, peace and love. And none of these can be obtained without first giving them to someone else. And, oh, how he gave for so many years!

He is indeed a legend in basketball but more importantly he was a legend in serving humankind as a master teacher. Hall of Fame sportscaster Dick Enberg said, "Coach Wooden's greatness was exceeded only by his goodness."

Now that Coach Wooden has left this earth, I ask myself: How can I ever thank him for being my friend for 40 years? And, as usual, my answer comes from the words of Coach himself. In the last letter I received from him, he wrote:

"Although 'thanks' is a rather simple, one-syllable word that too often is used without true feeling, when used with sincerity no collection of words can be more meaningful or expressive."

Coach Wooden was asked how he would like to be remembered, and he replied simply: "As a normal person who was considerate of others."

I would agree with that wholeheartedly, if by "considerate" one understands that Coach was unselfish, kind, charitable and sensitive, to mention but a few of his virtues.

And to that, I would add my own firsthand experiences with him. After spending time together, each time I left him I felt better, more optimistic about the human race, and I was motivated to strive to be a better man.

Perhaps the best way to remember Coach Wooden would be reflected in the immortal words of Albert Einstein in describing Mahatma Gandhi:

"Generations to come will scarce believe that such a one as this ever in flesh and blood walked upon this earth."

# Index

# Index of Key Phrases

# Sources

Angers, Trent. *Dale Brown Court: and the Battle for Human Dignity*. Lafayette, La.: Acadian House Publishing, 2023.

Baldwin, James. *Nobody Knows My Name*. New York: The Dial Press, 1961.

Brown, Coach Dale. *Getting Over the Four Hurdles of Life*. Lafayette, La.: Acadian House Publishing, 2011.

Donne, John. *Devotions Upon Emergent Occasions*. London: The Stationers' Company, January 1624.

Dossey, Larry. *Healing Words: The Power of Prayer and the Practice of Medicine*. New York: Harper Collins, 1993.

Frankl, Viktor. *Man's Search for Meaning*. Boston: Beacon Press, 1962.

Guest, Edgar A. *Collected Verse of Edgar A. Guest*. Chicago: Reilly & Lee, 1934.

James, William. *The Principles of Psychology*. New York: Henry Holt & Co., 1890.

King Jr., Martin Luther. "Letter from a Birmingham Jail." August 1963.
– "Give Us the Ballot." Speech, Prayer Pilgrimage for Freedom, Washington, D.C., May 17, 1957.
– "Some Things We Must Do." Speech, Holt Street Baptist Church, Montgomery, Ala., December 5, 1957.

Lincoln, Abraham. "Address Before the Young Men's Lyceum of Springfield, Illinois." Speech, Young Men's Lyceum, Springfield, Ill., January 27, 1838.

Mandela, Nelson. "Release from Prison Address." Speech, Cape Town, South Africa, February 11, 1990.
– *Long Walk to Freedom*. Johannesburg, South Africa: Macdonald Purnell Ltd., 1994.

Shakespeare, William. *Hamlet*. London: First Folio, 1623.

Thoreau, Henry David. *Walden*. Boston: Ticknor and Fields, 1854.

Wooden, Coach John. *Wooden: A Lifetime of Observations and Reflections On and Off the Court*. New York: McGraw-Hill, 1997.

# About the Author ...

**COACH DALE BROWN,** who served as head coach of the LSU men's basketball team for 25 years (1972 - 1997), is recognized as one of the all-time best motivational speakers in the U.S.

Widely known as the nation's leading advocate of NCAA reform, he successfully campaigned for 35 years to change or eliminate dozens of rules in the NCAA rule book, which governs student-athletes nationwide.

As LSU coach, he was twice named National Basketball Coach of the Year, led his teams to two Final Fours and four Elite Eights, and emerged as the second-winningest coach in SEC history. Having won 448 games, he retired as the winningest men's basketball coach in LSU history, and in 2014 was inducted into the National Collegiate Basketball Hall of Fame.

He lives in Baton Rouge, La., with his wife, Vonnie.

---

**TRENT ANGERS**, nominated twice for the Nobel Prize in Literature (2000 and 2001), is a veteran journalist who has authored countless published news and feature stories, as well as seven books, in a writing and editing career that has spanned five decades.

His better known-known books are *The Forgotten Hero of My Lai: The Hugh Thompson Story* (1999 and 2014); *Grand Coteau: The Holy Land of South Louisiana* (2004); *The Truth About the Cajuns* (1989); and *Dale Brown Court: ... and the Battle for Human Dignity* (2023).

A second-generation journalist who grew up in the newspaper business, he is a 1970 graduate of the LSU School of Journalism, and for 36 years was editor and publisher of *Acadiana Profile*, "The Magazine of the Cajun Country." He is a member of the Secular Franciscan Order and resides in Lafayette, La.

# Inspiring Books
from
# Acadian House Publishing

## The Little Book of Motivation

A compact 112-page hardcover book packed with inspiring messages from one of America's top motivational speakers, former LSU basketball coach Dale Brown. The book is, essentially, a written version of some of Brown's most memorable speeches. Themes include courage, integrity, leadership, tolerance and teamwork. The author describes proven ways of achieving happiness, success and peace of mind. (Author: Coach Dale Brown, the "Master Motivator." ISBN: 979-8-9896580-8-4. Price $15.00.)

## Getting Over the 4 Hurdles of Life

A 160-page softcover book that shows us ways to get past the obstacles, or hurdles, that block our path to success, happiness and peace of mind. Four of the most common hurdles are "I can't / You can't," past failures or fear of failure, handicaps, and lack of self-knowledge. This inspiring book – by one of the top motivational speakers in the U.S. – is brought to life by intriguing stories of various people who overcame life's hurdles. Introduction by former LSU and NBA star Shaquille O'Neal. (Author: Coach Dale Brown. ISBN: 0-925417-83-1. Price: $14.95)

## Tiger Beat

*Covering LSU sports for 35 years*

A 240-page hardcover book by a veteran sportswriter who covered LSU football and basketball for Baton Rouge, La., newspapers for 35 years. It features the head coaches over a 50-year span, starting in the mid-1950s, as well as big games and top athletes, including the "Chinese Bandits," Billy Cannon, "Pistol Pete" Maravich, Chris Jackson and Shaquille O'Neal. (Author: Sam King. ISBN: 0-925417-85-8. Price $22.95)

## Dale Brown Court

### *... and the Battle for Human Dignity*

The 296-page biography of legendary LSU basketball coach Dale Brown, focusing on his role as leader of the successful decades-long campaign to reform the NCAA rule book. Proclaiming for years that "the NCAA legislates against human dignity," his tireless efforts are today benefiting some 500,000 student-athletes per year across the U.S. – making him a true national hero. A civil rights leader and humanitarian, Brown was finally honored when the LSU basketball court was named for him in 2021. The book provides a behind-the-scenes look into the years-long struggle to have the court named in his honor. (Author: Trent Angers. Hardcover ISBN: 979-8-9864600-4-8. Price: $26.00 Softcover ISBN: 979-8-9864600-7-9. Price: $18.00)

## Everything Matters in Baseball

### *The Skip Bertman Story*

A 248-page hardcover biography of legendary LSU baseball coach Skip Bertman, one of America's most successful college coaches. The book reveals Bertman's "Secrets to Success" and gives detailed reports on his five National Championships. It portrays him as a true master of the positive mental attitude, a staunch advocate of hard work, and a stickler for detail. It also describes his stint as LSU's Athletics Director. Foreword by baseball superstar Warren Morris. Illustrated with 32 pages of photos. (Author: Glenn Guilbeau. ISBN: 978-1-7352641-4-1. Price: $30.00)

## From Bags to Riches

### *How the New Orleans Saints and the people of their hometown rose from the depths together*

The inspiring story of the New Orleans Saints' 2009-2010 football season that culminated with the winning of the Super Bowl. The book explains how the struggling NFL team and the storm-weary people of New Orleans and the Gulf Coast lifted one another's spirits – and fortunes – in the post-Hurricane Katrina years, 2006 – 2010. The narrative is a study in contrasting moods, ranging from the depression and despair that come with being victims of the worst natural disaster in U.S. history, to the euphoria that accompanies the winning of the Super Bowl after 43 years of mostly losing seasons. (Author: Jeff Duncan ISBN: 0-925417-68-8. Price: $24.95)

## Freedom From Fear

***A Way Through The Ways of Jesus The Christ***

Everyone at one time or another feels fear, guilt, worry and shame. But when these emotions get out of control they can enslave a person, literally taking over his or her life. In this 142-page softcover book, the author suggests that the way out of this bondage is prayer, meditation and faith in God and His promise of salvation. The author points to the parables in the Gospels as Jesus' antidote to fears of various kinds, citing the parables of the prodigal son, the good Samaritan, and the widow and the judge. Exercises at the end of each chapter help make the book's lessons all the more real and useful. (Author: Francis Vanderwall. ISBN: 0-925417-34-3. Price: $14.95)

## God First (Book 2)

***Walking in Faith***

A 144-page hardcover book designed to strengthen Christians in their journey of faith. The author points out that Christians are uniquely gifted, uniquely positioned, and uniquely equipped to help others in their search for a deeper, more meaningful relationship with Jesus Christ. The book emphasizes the necessity of trusting God, it offers an explanation of what tithing means to God, and it lays out ways to build one's faith community. (Author: Bryan G. Sibley, M.D. ISBN: 979-8-9896580-0-8. Price $16.00)

## What They Don't Teach You in Catholic College

***Women in the priesthood and the mind of Christ***

A 216-page hardcover book that makes the case for women in the Catholic priesthood – even though the hierarchy of the Church has traditionally opposed the idea, based largely on their belief that Christ wanted a male-only priesthood for all time. The author, a renowned theologian, disputes that ultra-conservative viewpoint and explains why it is in the Church's best interest to ordain women. (Author: John Wijngaards, DD, LSS. ISBN: 0-9995884-4-3. Price $16.95, hardcover.)

## Leadership in the New Normal

### *A Short Course*

A 184-page softcover book on how to be an effective leader in the 21st century. It describes modern leadership principles and techniques and illustrates them with stories from the author's life experiences. He emerged as a national hero and one of the U.S.'s best-known military leaders in 2005 after spearheading the post-Hurricane Katrina search-and-rescue mission in New Orleans. (Author: General Russel Honoré. ISBN: 978-0925417-75-6. Price $16.00)

## Don't get stuck on stupid!

An insightful, thought-provoking book by the 3-star general who led the post-Hurricane Katrina search-and-rescue mission in New Orleans in 2005. General Russel Honoré offers effective solutions to some of the most pressing problems of our time: hurricane preparedness, healthcare, gun control, widespread infrastructure failure, and the need to intervene in the infamous cradle-to-prison pipeline. His basic message: It's time to try new ways to solve our problems. *Let's not continue to make the same mistakes with public policy and practice in our country... let's not get stuck on stupid!* (Author: General Russel Honore. ISBN: 0-999588-41-9. Paperback price $18.00)

## The Forgotten Hero of My Lai

### *The Hugh Thompson Story* (Revised Edition)

The 272-page softcover book that tells the story of the U.S. Army helicopter pilot who risked his life to rescue South Vietnamese civilians and to put a stop to the My Lai massacre during the Vietnam War in 1968. Revised Edition shows President Nixon initiated the effort to sabotage the My Lai massacre trials so no U.S. soldier would be convicted of a war crime. (Author: Trent Angers. ISBN: 979-8-9864600-2-4. Price: $17.95)

## The Elephant Man

### *A Study in Human Dignity*

The Elephant Man is a 138-page softcover book whose first edition inspired the movie and the Tony Award-winning play by the same name. This fascinating story, which has touched the hearts of readers throughout the world for over a century, is now complete with the publication of this, the Third Edition. Illustrated with photos and drawings of The Elephant Man. (Author: Ashley Montagu. ISBN: 0-925417-41-6. Price: $14.95.)

## Infused

### *My Story of Cancer, Hope and Love*

A 208-page hardcover autobiography of a young Austin, Texas, woman and her 5-year battle with breast cancer. The narrative takes us from her original diagnosis (only 3 months after she was married) through her search for the right doctor, chemotherapy, mastectomies, and the birth of her child by way of a surrogate. Written in a lively and very informative voice, the story is infused with hope, inspiration, and wit, with an extra dose of sarcasm. (Author: Courtney Bax Lasater, ISBN 0-925417-21-1. Price $22.95)

## An Airboat on the Streets of New Orleans

### *A Cajun couple lends a hand after Hurricane Katrina floods the city*

A 192-page book about a Cajun couple from Breaux Bridge, La., who took their airboat into New Orleans when the city flooded as a result of Hurricane Katrina. Doug Bienvenu, the airboat operator, and Drue LeBlanc, who was suffering with kidney disease, rescued hundreds of people during their 3-day mission of mercy. (Author: Trent Angers. Hardcover ISBN: 0-925417-87-4. Price: $16.95. Softcover ISBN: 0-925417-88-2. Price: $14.95)

---

**TO ORDER,** list the books you wish to purchase along with the corresponding cost of each. For shipping in the U.S., add $4 for the first book, and $1 per book thereafter. For shipping out of the U.S., email us at info@acadianhouse.com for a price quote. Louisiana residents add 9% tax to the cost of the books. Mail your order and check or credit card authorization (VISA/MC/AmEx) to: Acadian House Publishing, P.O. Box 52247, Lafayette, LA 70505. Or call (337) 235-8851.

To order online, go to **www.acadianhouse.com.**